EXTREME WEATHER

Tsunamis

by Anne Wendorff

BELLWETHER MEDIA • MINNEAPOLIS, MN

Note to Librarians, Teachers, and Parents:

Blastoff! Readers are carefully developed by literacy experts and combine standards-based content with developmentally appropriate text.

Level 1 provides the most support through repetition of high-frequency words, light text, predictable sentence patterns, and strong visual support.

Level 2 offers early readers a bit more challenge through varied simple sentences, increased text load, and less repetition of high-frequency words.

Level 3 advances early-fluent readers toward fluency through increased text and concept load, less reliance on visuals, longer sentences, and more literary language.

Level 4 builds reading stamina by providing more text per page, increased use of punctuation, greater variation in sentence patterns, and increasingly challenging vocabulary.

Level 5 encourages children to move from "learning to read" to "reading to learn" by providing even more text, varied writing styles, and less familiar topics.

Whichever book is right for your reader, Blastoff! Readers are the perfect books to build confidence and encourage a love of reading that will last a lifetime!

This edition first published in 2009 by Bellwether Media.

No part of this publication may be reproduced in whole or in part without written permission of the publisher. For information regarding permission, write to Bellwether Media Inc., Attention: Permissions Department, Post Office Box 19349, Minneapolis, MN 55419.

Library of Congress Cataloging-in-Publication Data
Wendorff, Anne.
  Tsunamis / by Anne Wendorff.
    p. cm. – (Blastoff! readers. Extreme weather)
  Summary: "Simple text and full color photographs introduce beginning readers to the characteristics of tsunamis. Developed by literacy experts for students in kindergarten through third grade"–Provided by publisher.
  Includes bibliographical references and index.
  ISBN-13: 978-1-60014-188-1 (hardcover : alk. paper)
  ISBN-10: 1-60014-188-9 (hardcover : alk. paper)
  1. Tsunamis–Juvenile literature. I. Title.

GC221.5.W46 2009
551.46'37–dc22   2008015222

Contents

What Is a Tsunami?

Waves move constantly on the ocean. Ordinary waves are caused by the wind pushing water. Sometimes a far more powerful kind of wave forms.

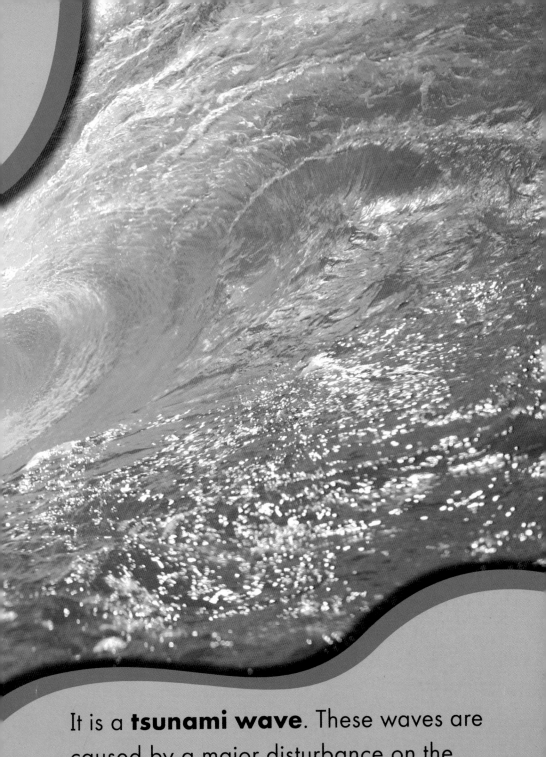

It is a **tsunami wave**. These waves are caused by a major disturbance on the ocean floor, such as an **earthquake**.

How Do Tsunamis Form?

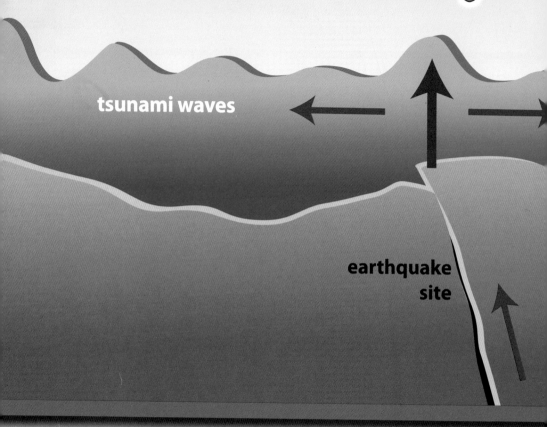

tsunami waves

earthquake site

Underwater earthquakes shake up the ocean floor. This movement can send waves traveling in all directions. Each wave is called a tsunami wave.

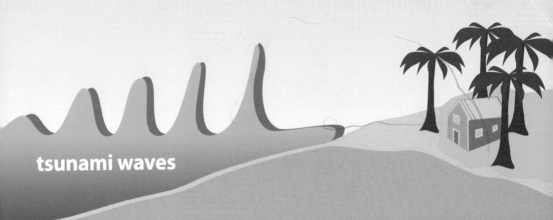

tsunami waves

Most tsunamis are caused by earthquakes, but any disturbance in the ocean floor can cause one. Underwater **volcanic eruptions** and **mudslides** can also cause tsunamis.

A tsunami in the open ocean is not very noticeable. This is because the open ocean is usually very deep. Most of the power of a tsunami is below the ocean's surface.

Some tsunamis lose energy and die out. Others travel great distances across the ocean.

Near the shore, the ocean floor rises. As a tsunami wave approaches the shore, the rising ocean floor pushes up on it. This causes the tsunami wave to grow taller.

fast fact

Just before a tsunami wave hits land, the ocean water will often pull away from shore, uncovering the ocean floor. This is caused by the dip in water level in front of a wave.

A tsunami wave can rise over 100 feet (30 meters) in shallow water. It looks like a giant wall of water as it approaches land.

What Can Tsunamis Do?

Tsunami waves can move at speeds up to 500 miles (804.5 kilometers) per hour. This is as fast as some jet planes. They can cause massive destruction when they hit land. The waves can smash buildings near the shore.

Tsunamis can crash into land with huge force. Waves can smash houses, uproot trees, and pull people out to sea. Tsunamis often cause destruction far beyond the shoreline. They have caused flooding as far as a half mile (0.8 kilometers) inland.

Measuring and Predicting Tsunamis

Scientists rank tsunamis by the height of their waves and the amount of damage they cause. The largest tsunamis have waves over 52 feet (16 meters) tall.

Large tsunamis cause severe flooding and destroy nearly every building in their path. A smaller tsunami can have waves as little as 6 feet (2 meters) high and may cause little damage.

Predicting tsunamis is difficult. It is hard
to predict underwater disturbances
and not every disturbance causes a
tsunami. Recently, scientists placed
special **buoys** in some ocean areas.
These help detect and track tsunamis.

Predicting a tsunami is only the first step. Scientists also want to warn people in its path. This is also difficult because tsunamis move quickly in every direction.

The Indian Ocean Tsunami

On December 26th, 2004, an earthquake caused a major tsunami in the Indian Ocean. Tsunami waves spread throughout the area. The worst waves hit parts of Southeast Asia. They crashed into coastal areas.

Many people were pulled out to sea. In all, more than 200,000 people were killed. Millions were left homeless. This was one of the most destructive tsunamis in history. Today, scientists work hard to protect people from tsunamis that may happen in the future.

Glossary

buoys—floating objects placed in the ocean; some buoys gather data that helps scientists predict tsunamis.

earthquake—a sudden movement of the earth's crust; undersea earthquakes are the leading cause of tsunamis.

mudslide—a flow of mud on the ocean floor; undersea mudslides are one cause of tsunamis.

tsunami wave—an ocean wave caused by an underground disturbance such as an earthquake; tsunamis can be huge and very fast.

volcanic eruption—the eruption of magma onto the earth's crust; underwater volcanic eruptions are one cause of tsunamis.

To Learn More

AT THE LIBRARY
Berger, Melvin and Gilda. *What Makes an Ocean Wave?* New York: Scholastic Reference, 2001.

Morrison, Taylor. *Tsunami Warning*. New York: Houghton Mifflin, 2007.

Woods, Michael and Mary. *Tsunamis*. Minneapolis, Minn.: Lerner, 2007.

ON THE WEB
Learning more about tsunamis is as easy as 1, 2, 3.

1. Go to www.factsurfer.com

2. Enter "tsunamis" into search box.

3. Click the "Surf" button and you will see a list of related web sites.

With factsurfer.com, finding more information is just a click away.

Index

The images in this book are reproduced through the courtesy of: Fouquin, front cover; Mana Photo, pp. 4-5, 12-13; Linda Clavel, pp. 6-7; Alexey Stiop, pp. 8, 9; 2005 AFP / Getty Images, pp. 10-11, 14; Stephen J. Boitano / Alamy, p.16; Juan Martinez, p.18; George Clerk, p.19; ImageForum / Getty Images, pp. 20, 21.